SCHOOL SURVIVAL

KATE TYM AND PENNY WORMS

Raintree

Chicago, Illinois

For information, address the publisher:
Raintree, 100 N. LaSalle, Suite 1200, Chicago, IL 60602

Produced for Raintree by Ticktock Media Ltd.

Photography by Roddy Payne Photographic Studio

Printed and bound in China by South China Printing Company.

09 08 07 06 05
10 9 8 7 6 5 4 3 2 1

Library of Congress Cataloging-in-Publication Data
Tym, Kate.
   School survival / Kate Tym and Penny Worms.
      p. cm. -- (Get real)
   Includes index.
   ISBN 1-4109-0577-2
   1. Socialization--Juvenile literature. 2. School environment--Juvenile literature. 3. Peer pressure--Juvenile
literature. I. Worms, Penny. II. Title. III. Series: Tym, Kate. Get real.
   LC192.4.T96 2005
   371.8'019--dc22
                           2004008070

Acknowledgments
The publisher would like to thank the following for permission to reproduce copyright materials:
Alamy: pp. **18–19** center, **22** top, **23** center, **25** top, **28** top, **30–31** center, **31** top, **32** top, **34** top, **38** top, **39** top. Comstock: p. **29**. Digital Vision: pp. **4** top, **4–5** center, **5** bottom, **6–7** bottom, **16** top, **19** top, **31** top, **36** top, **43** top. Photodisc: p. **7** top. Roddy Payne Photographic Studio: pp. **8** top, **9** top, **10** top, **11**, **14** top, **15** top, **17**, **18** top, **20** top, **21** top, **26** top, **35**, **40** top. Stockbyte: pp. **12–13** center, **13** top, **24–25** center, **27** top, **33** top, **36–37** center, **41**, **42** top, **42–43** center.

Front cover photograph by Alamy, back cover photograph by Stockbyte.

Every effort has been made to contact copyright holders of any material reproduced in this book. Any omissions will be rectified in subsequent printings if notice is given to the publisher.

• CONTENTS • CONTENTS • CONTENTS •

INTRODUCTION

SCHOOL DAYS

School days can be the best days of your life—or can they?
Why is it that many people experience difficulties during those years?

"I wish I could go back to school. I'd try harder."

Exam stress, parent pressure, peer pressure, or boredom can come as a bit of a shock after the fun-filled days of elementary school. Yes, you'll get through, but will you come out the other side with good experiences, good grades, and good friends? Or will you suffer from study-induced burnout, could-have-done-better results, or find yourself on the outside of your "in" crowd? There's no doubt about it, school presents the ideal environment for at least one or two tough lessons in life.

School is a hierarchical institution: with the principal at the top, teachers next, and students descending down the pecking order in accordance with age. And then, within each year group there can be a battle for power, popularity, or success. If you're bright, have lots of friends, and the support of your family, your school days can be stimulating and enjoyable. But if you're struggling with work, discipline issues, or find it hard fitting in, then school can seem like a living nightmare. It does not have to be all doom and gloom!

"I want a good education, but I want to have a good time, too."

School is also a place full of opportunities and new experiences. It's the place where you are independent of your family, and where you begin to forge your way in the world and make lifelong friends. It's where you learn lessons—not only about the world, but also about yourself, other people, and how to relate to them. You continue to establish attitudes and ideas of your own, learn how to take responsibility, and how to stand on your own two feet. Another great thing about school is it's temporary! Whatever trials you are facing at school, there is an end to them. Like everything in life, you'll get through them and they will soon become a distant memory—whether good or bad. In the meantime though, there are lots of strategies to employ so those shark-infested waters of school are just a little bit easier to sail through.

This book covers various aspects of school life. It includes true-life experiences, excellent advice, and top tips to help you cope. Even if the experiences don't directly relate to you, they will help you realize that whatever the issue, you're probably not alone and . . . there's always a way to sort it out. If stress isn't your problem, then maybe boredom is. How are you supposed to concentrate on a subject that makes your brain shut down or a teacher who doesn't inspire you?

OUR EXPERT PANEL
THE EXPERTS GIVING ADVICE ARE . . .

Anita Jardine
Anita Jardine is the parent of two teenagers and is an experienced family practitioner. She is currently employed as a school counselor and is involved in providing a solution-focused service for young people and their parents/care givers.

Simon Howell
Simon Howell is a social worker and family therapist.

Mac Buckley
Mac Buckley is a family case worker. She has worked in residential homes, schools, and family centers for children and young people.

CASE STUDIES
Within each chapter are case studies— true stories about real people who have had some kind of problem to overcome. Read their stories, check out the experts' advice, and learn what actually happened in the end. All the names of the contributors have been changed to protect their identity, and models have been used for the photographs.

EXAM STRESS-BUSTERS

EXAMS ARE STRESSFUL BUT THERE ARE WAYS TO HELP YOU THROUGH . . .

- **Be prepared**
  If you know your stuff, you've got nothing to worry about, have you?

- **Take deep breaths**
  When you sit down and feel that adrenaline-rush, breathe in and out slowly three times. You'll be amazed at the calming effect this can have.

- **Take your time**
  You may feel that time is against you, and that you need to rush to get through everything. But taking a moment at the beginning of the exam to gather your thoughts will pay dividends in the end. If you take the time to compose yourself and read the instructions and questions carefully, it will mean no last-minute crisis when you realize you read the question wrong in the first place.

- **Do the things you can cope with most easily first**
  Tackle the questions you know you can do and you'll buy a bit of time to deal with the more taxing questions later . . . by which time you'll probably be feeling a bit calmer, too.

EDUCATION, EDUCATION

IT'S WHAT YOU GO TO SCHOOL FOR

Although some people treat lessons as the boring part of an otherwise enjoyable day with their friends, to a major extent lessons are why you go to school.

The theory of school is that you will be educated and come out of school with a basic knowledge of all the things you'll need to get by in the world. But to you, it may seem like an endless stream of work, exams, and lessons that seem pointless. Why learn about land irrigation when you want to be a soccer player or a fashion designer? But what if you don't make it as a soccer player or designer? Your education gives you choices and enables you to go down a different road to success.

> "Why do we have to learn such dull stuff."

At the other end of the scale, you may see school as a constant pressure to do well. It is usually a competitive environment and if you have the teachers on your case and your parents on your back, it's no wonder you feel stressed! A certain amount of work stress can be helpful—it motivates you to get things done—but too much stress can be bad. Living up to other people's expectations of you and the nagging worry that you might blow your future can at times seem overwhelming.

"My parents would be disappointed if I messed up."

If you feel under too much pressure, it's important to find a balance and a way of working that's right for you. Seek help when you need it and don't forget that all work and no play leads directly to serious burnout. To get the best out of these years at school, you need to work to your full ability at school and with homework, so you can spend the rest of your time worry-free and doing what you enjoy.

4 STUDY TOP TIPS

If you're prepared for an exam or test, you stand more chance of doing well. So just how should you prepare?

1. PREPARE AS YOU WOULD FOR A VACATION

How do you prepare for a vacation? You think about what you need, you go shopping for things you don't have, and you're amazed at how much stuff you've packed into a small suitcase. Apply the same amount of effort to exams and your brain will be stuffed with the facts you need.

2. START STUDYING EARLY

Yawn! Yes, you know the theory, but there are friends to meet and you can study tomorrow, right? Well, just as you're about to say this to yourself one more time, think about this . . . your brain works better if you take breaks in between study sessions. So start the studying today. Then go out, and come back refreshed.

3. STUDY WITH FRIENDS

Take an hour to focus on what you need to learn and help one another to understand. Then you've got the rest of the time for fun.

4. TRY DIFFERENT STUDY METHODS

Try reading and recording facts on tape or dictaphone. Because you are using more of your senses, your brain is more engaged. You can also play it back to yourself in the bath or in bed.

7

IT'S SOMETHING I'VE GOT TO GET THROUGH

Claire, 15, views school as boring and useless. Her attendance is slipping . . .

> "The teachers don't do anything to make it interesting—they just get us to copy from the board."

I find school really boring. The teachers don't do anything to make it interesting. They just get us to copy from the board or from books.

And it's all really strict, but over stupid stuff. Like you're not allowed to wear hoop earrings— just one pair of studs— and the boys can't have long hair. You can't even dye your hair or have your nose or eyebrow pierced.

You get detention if you're two seconds late. What does that do anyway? Sitting in a room for half an hour, big deal—it's not like you learn anything from that. My attendance hasn't been that great. I haven't wanted to do much since my parents split up, and it's not like the school are interested. I mean I understand that you should do well at school and everything if you want to get a good job, but I see it as something I have got to get through.

ASK THE EXPERTS...

Simon the social worker says . . .
While some people love school, for others it's a real drag. If you don't naturally enjoy the work, it is easy to be distracted, especially when you are going through something as difficult as your parents breaking up. I can understand that you want to be an individual, but try to modify your dress while you are at school. You can still wear your piercings on the weekend, when you can really show how cool you are!

Anita the counselor says . . .
It can be difficult carrying on with your usual routine after something as big as your parents splitting up. What seem like petty rules can become even more frustrating when you're at a stage of wanting to express your individuality. But the rules are set to take the pressure off those who feel differently or who can't afford to follow the latest trends.

Mac the family case worker says . . .
It's hard when you have to deal with such big issues. It's natural to feel hurt and angry, and to want to rebel. But who's it really hurting? You. Try not to fight the system all the time. Keep your hoop earrings for the weekends. And remember, a good time-keeping habit will help to get you that great job one day. School isn't forever!

NOTHING SEEMS TO GO IN

Meredith, 14, finds it stressful keeping on top of her schoolwork.

I do like school but I find it quite difficult to cope with all the work. Not just homework, but in class, too. I seem to have to work harder than all my friends.

It makes me stressed when I see that they have done more work than me. I start feeling like I haven't done enough and panic. My mom's quite strict—she won't let me go out till I've done my homework. I get piles of it and I usually do it as soon as I get in from school, because if I don't get it done it really preys on my mind and I get really stressed out. If I haven't done it by Friday, I don't usually

> "I get distracted and end up doing nothing. Then I feel bad because I've wasted time."

go out. I can't stand to have it hanging around for the weekend. When we've got exams, I try to study hard but half the time nothing seems to go in. I just sit in my room and think, "Okay. I'll get started." Usually I get distracted and end up doing nothing. Then I feel really bad because I've wasted all this time and I've got to study again tomorrow.

ASK THE EXPERTS...

Simon the social worker says . . . When work keeps on coming like this we can feel like a hamster in a tread-wheel running without end. And if you like to do a good job that's added pressure. But it's the quality of your homework that really matters, not the quantity. And that means spending quality time on it. Negotiate a new schedule with yourself and your mom that allows you to work when you're fresh and play when you need to.

Anita the counselor says . . . You're obviously very conscientious about getting your work done, but sometimes the worrying gets in the way. Your mom sounds supportive in helping you stick to a routine, knowing your stress will decrease once you have done the work. It is good that you manage to leave yourself some free time on the weekend after you've done your work and can relax and enjoy it.

Mac the family case worker says . . . Tackling homework and exams is as much about having a system as the amount of time it takes. Try five minutes relaxation as soon as you get home from school. Put on some music, lie down, and think of a "happy place" where you don't feel stressed. When you study, learn a manageable chunk one evening, re-learn it two days later, then read it again at the end of the week.

THEY'VE GIVEN UP TRYING

Theo, 14, is glad because no one gets on his case about school anymore. He's just not interested.

> "Why can't we learn interesting things like car mechanics or game programming?"

My dad and my teachers have stopped giving me a hard time about school. They know it won't do any good because basically I'm just too cool for school.

Studying is for geeks and girls. My teachers don't really care anyway. All they do is tell me off, even if it's not my fault. Other boys in my class could be goofing around and I'm the one who gets shouted at. I don't see the point in me taking tests. It's not as if I'm ever going to surprise them by suddenly getting an "A." Life's too short to worry about stuff like that. Why can't we learn interesting things like car mechanics or game programming? That I'd be interested in—I might even get an A! Then I'd get respect. But in the real world, people will respect me, that's for sure.

ASK THE EXPERTS...

Simon the social worker says . . .
A lot of students are interested in learning practical skills rather than studying. Schools may not teach exactly what you want to learn. It's great that you know what you want to do. The problem is doing well enough in school so you can get where you want in the future. Choose subjects that are most like your interests and get the most you can out of them.

Anita the counselor says . . .
You seem to be full of confidence and sure that academia is not for you. Sometimes you can get a "reputation" at school which means you get the blame when others goof around, which can seem really unfair. You may be able to choose more suitable subjects when you choose your options next year—it sounds as if you have practical skills that you're keen to develop.

Mac the family case worker says . . .
Car mechanics and programmers need diplomas, too. It's great to be cool, but not if you're unemployed! People will respect you if you try and you're a good person to have around. So try making an effort—you'll be surprised to find there are things you're really good at and options that might really suit you. People will admire your determination far more than your "couldn't care less" attitude.

THE OUTCOMES

After reading our experts' advice, Claire, Meredith, and Theo wrote back to let us know how things turned out . . .

GET CONNECTED

Children's Rights Council
2201 I ("Eye") Street
Suite 200
Washington, D.C. 20002
The CRC assists children of separation and divorce through advocacy and parenting education.

CASE STUDY 1

Consider the options

My parents break-up was hard but things have settled down a bit. I'm at school every day now. I found it was more boring at home! My attitude to school hasn't changed— I still see it as something I've got to get through —but if I've got to be here I suppose I might as well make the most of it. I do want a job that pays well when I leave.

CASE STUDY 2

Relax!

I guess I'm a worrier—that's just part of being me. I need people to give me confidence, but they can't be with me in an exam so I'm going to do my best to prepare beforehand. I know I'll still worry but if I've done enough work, I should be able to feel better about it. I'm trying the relaxing thing, too. I never thought that lying down and resting for five minutes might help me study! And setting a time to stop, too, has helped because I plan what I want to watch on TV when I'm done.

CASE STUDY 3

Don't give up on yourself

I don't think it's fair that people expect more from girls and give them more attention. They've all written me off but I'm no loser. I'm not going to be unemployed when I leave school. No way. I can't buy my Mercedes on unemployment benefits! My friend told me that he's going to drop the boring subjects next year and do woodwork and art. That sounds more my thing. I guess I'd better check out what else I can do. He also told me about his brother who is only sixteen and he's at college. That sounds all right.

REMEMBER
- Relaxation, sleep, and exercise all help you study!
- Whether you love or loathe school, don't come out with nothing to show for it.
- Discuss any worries with your teachers or parents. Don't be afraid to ask for help.
- Plan your time. Whether it's an hour's homework or two weeks of studying.
- If you do well in school, you'll have more job options when you leave.

11

SCHOOL FRIENDS

FROM BONDING TO BUST-UPS

School is packed full of potential friends. Some might turn into friends for life, while others could be stepping stones toward other people with whom you will form deeper bonds.

Having friends can make or break the whole school experience for you. Remember your first week at school—knowing few, if any, people? You probably felt insecure, uncomfortable, and quite lonely. Compare that to walking into school today. You have friends to gravitate to, talk to, and be with. Friendships help you learn about who you are, and about the qualities that matter in human relationships. You can share things with friends that you might not be able to share with your family, not to mention having like-minded people around to have a laugh (or cry) with!

Some friendships are deep and meaningful, while others might be more casual and light-hearted. Making friends is not easy for everyone, but there are times when we all have to do it— and it doesn't get any harder than joining a new school.

"My friends are such fun. They make school bearable."

HOW TO SPOT A TRUE FRIEND

Some friendships are high-maintenance and learning how to recognize the good from the bad, and deal with them accordingly, is quite a skill. But you know you've got a true friend if . . .

- **You enjoy each other's company**
- **You feel loyal toward each other**
- **You're always there for each other**
- **You like each other just as you are**
- **You're not dependent on each other**
- **You talk honestly**
- **You laugh together**
- **You trust each other**

But if you're confident (even if you're a bundle of nerves inside), approachable, and chatty, you will quickly get to know people and eventually you'll find those friends you click with. A more long-term problem of school life is maintaining the friendships you've got. One week you could be best buddies. The next you've fallen out. Most friends make up quickly, but bitter arguments, gossip, and harsh words can lead to a friendship nightmare. Suddenly all the security you felt by having your friends is whipped away and you're left feeling isolated and unsure of yourself, just like your first day at school. Having a wide circle of friends is the way to avoid this from ever happening to you. Having time for more than one group is not only more interesting, but it means you are not dependent on the whims of others. Your popularity goes beyond that.

TOP TIPS FOR STAYING FRIENDS

- **IF YOU WANT GREAT, HASSLE-FREE FRIENDSHIPS . . .**
  treat your friends the way you'd like them to treat you.

- **IF YOU'RE FINDING A FRIEND HARD TO GET ALONG WITH . . .**
  don't talk behind their back.

- **IF YOU STRESS ABOUT WHO IS BEST FRIENDS WITH WHO . . .**
  lighten up. Having a best friend can be wonderful, but having lots of supportive friends is great, too.

- **IF YOU GET JEALOUS OF YOUR BEST FRIEND'S OTHER FRIENDS . . .**
  remember you're both entitled to have other friends. It doesn't mean you like each other less.

- **IF YOU DO ARGUE . . .**
  don't be too proud to say sorry.

- **IF A FRIEND TELLS YOU A SECRET AND ASKS YOU NOT TO TELL ANYONE . . .**
  then that's exactly what you should do. And no it's not okay to tell "just one" other person!

- **IF YOU ARGUE OVER A GIRLFRIEND/BOYFRIEND . . .**
  you're not thinking straight. Your friends will be around long after the girlfriend/boyfriend.

"Suddenly I was like a new kid with no one to go to lunch with."

13

CASE STUDY 1

WHAT AM I GOING TO DO WITHOUT HER?

"What if we end up drifting apart? I couldn't bear that!"

Pamu, 11, is worried about starting her new school next year. How is she going to face it without her best friend?

I'm starting a new school in September and my best friend, Grace, is going to a different one. I don't know what I'm going to do without her.

She's just everything you'd want in a friend and I won't find another friend like her. She's always there for me—pleased when nice things happen and sympathetic when stuff goes wrong. I can tell her everything. We always spend lots of time together and have even been on vacation with each other's families. She's not exactly like me—she has her own way of dressing and her own opinions and everything—but she understands what I'm like, and we have this totally in-tune sense of humor where we just have to give each other a look and we're in fits. In her new school, she's going to have to find a new best friend, and so am I, but what if we end up drifting apart? I couldn't bear that.

ASK THE EXPERTS...

Simon the social worker says . . .
Best friends are great because we share so much more with them. Day-to-day friends are just as important though. They make a positive difference every day. Changing schools is going to mean new places, new people, and new subjects. Your day-to-day friends will change. You may even get close to some of them, too. That doesn't mean you and your best friend can't carry on. Start planning now how you'll keep in touch.

Anita the counselor says . . .
It's always daunting, as well as exciting, starting at a new school. It sounds as though you and Grace have enjoyed a very special friendship, being able to share the highs as well as the lows. With such a close bond, I would be surprised if you two didn't manage to keep in touch and have even more to talk about living more separate lives. Being so valued will give you the confidence to make new friends wherever you go.

Mac the family case worker says . . .
It's great you've made such a good friend. You have a good positive example to judge new friends in the future. Perhaps you can join out-of-school clubs together so you still meet regularly, and you can always plan things on the weekends and during the holidays. You don't have to lose old friends when you change schools—you just need to make a little bit more effort, that's all!

GOSSIPING BROKE US UP

Maria, 14, is upset because her once close-knit group of friends has fallen apart because of gossiping.

I met Joanna in homeroom and she has been my best friend ever since. Then over time there were four of us and we moved up to high school together.

Everyone has started gossiping about each other and it's really horrible. One of the girls in our group, Shelly, seems to be playing us all off against each other. She's told Joanna that I've been saying things about her. At first Joanna didn't believe Shelly, but then she started to believe her and started saying nasty things behind my back in retaliation. Joanna started lying to me and I'd find out about it and confront her. This led to a series of arguments. We've grown apart a bit anyway—we're now quite different. I suppose I knew we wouldn't be best friends forever, but it's all seemed to happen so quickly. And now I feel really weird because suddenly I don't have a best friend anymore.

> "Everyone has started gossiping about each other and it's really horrible."

ASK THE EXPERTS...

Simon the social worker says . . .
A group of friends can be complicated. You can do more in a group and when everyone gets along it can be lots of fun. But it can become a nightmare if someone decides to change things for their own reasons. If your group is splitting apart, decide whether it is worth staying part of that group. Maybe it is time to look outside your circle to meet new people.

Anita the counselor says . . .
It isn't unusual for friendships to grow apart. Already your friendship with Joanna had moved over to accommodate a larger group, which is quite natural. It's very unpleasant when someone is stirring though and you can see that it's better to avoid being drawn into talking about people behind their backs. Although it's hard to lose an old friend, you'll find that there's more room in your life for others with more similar interests.

Mac the family case worker says . . .
Learning to deal with friendships and break-ups is part of growing up. The learning is in being up-front and honest without being confrontational. If something like this happens again, tell your friend what is worrying you and why you value your friendship as well as the things that annoy you. It can sometimes be better having a larger friendship group—it's less intense.

HE'S TURNED AGAINST ME

Sanjit, 13, is having trouble with a friend of his, who has not only turned against him, but is turning his other friends against him, too.

My friend Kelvin is behaving really bad toward me and there is just no reason. I can only put it down to jealousy.

I'm a hard worker because that's just the way I am. Kelvin just does as little as he can get away with. In science class, the teacher had left a question on the board. Everyone had started work but at that point, I was the only person writing. I'd written quite a bit and Kelvin started saying, "Go on Sanjit, write a bit more, write a bit more," and he just kept repeating it. I didn't say anything because I could see what he was doing and so could everyone else in the class. But if one person laughed it encouraged him to keep going. I knew I could rise above it but it still hurt. Kelvin's started hanging out with my other friend, Al, because they are in classes together. The other day Al just shrugged me off and I don't understand why. Why is this happening to me?

> "I knew I could rise above it but it still hurt."

ASK THE EXPERTS...

Simon the social worker says . . . Some friends enjoy making fun of each other. And sometimes it can be funny. Other times, people can be hurtful when they are stressed. But someone who constantly picks on you or tries to turn people against you isn't a friend at all. Talk to them about it if you think the friendship is worth saving. If not, look for new friends who will treat you properly. Get help from an adult if they hassle you.

Anita the counselor says . . . Kelvin is taking cheap shots at your expense, maybe because he lacks confidence himself. It must be hurtful if this is affecting your relationship with your other friend. If you can't talk to Kelvin about how his behavior is making you feel, perhaps you can get to the bottom of things with Al. He'll understand that you haven't done anything wrong and still value your friendship.

Mac the family case worker says . . . This is all about "good" friends and "bad" friends. Kelvin is envious because you're such a good worker. Maybe he realizes that he should be trying harder? Think about making some new friends who will value you more. It might be worth catching Kelvin on his own and asking him directly what his problem is. Perhaps it's just a misunderstanding that can be sorted out?

THE OUTCOMES

After reading our experts' advice, Pamu, Maria, and Sanjit wrote back to let us know how things turned out . . .

GET CONNECTED

American Counseling Association
5999 Stevenson Avenue
Alexandria, VA 22304

CASE STUDY 1

Don't worry

We've both started our new schools and it's not as bad as I thought it was going to be. Grace has got new friends and so have I, but we still see one another a lot and we get along just as well as we ever did. We tried mixing our friends, but it didn't really work so we just arrange to do things together. It's quite good really, because we can talk about problems wc have with our other friends and give each other advice and stuff. I can't imagine us ever arguing, but if we did, it would have to be over something major.

CASE STUDY 2

Friends are all around you

I'm still friends with Joanna, but I don't spend my time with her or talk to her in the same way anymore. And now at school I've made so many new friends. Before I was always with Joanna, but now I've got mixed groups of friends. At first it was a bit funny, but at the same time as I broke friends with Joanna, Shelly broke up with her best friend, Ali. So Ali and I paired up . . . but we made friends with other people, too.

People kept asking what had happened with Joanna and so I'd talk to them about it and end up with more friends in the end. I think Joanna's a bit bored now, just being with Shelly all the time. She finds it hard to mix with other people because she's quiet and shy, so in a way I feel lucky—at least I have enough confidence to make new friends.

CASE STUDY 3

Talk it through

Kelvin told Al things about me that were completely untrue. In the beginning Al didn't believe him but then it just built up more and more until he couldn't escape it. I didn't have a clue what was going on until Al told me to off go away day. When he told me what Kelvin had been saying, it was just completely beyond me why he would be like that. Al says it's jealousy. And actually, if that's the only way he can feel good about himself, then I really feel sorry for him.

REMEMBER
- *Having special friends is great. Having lots of friends is better.*
- *All friendships have their ups and downs. You may argue, but you'll probably make up again in no time.*
- *Recognize the "bad" friends for what they are. Value the "good" friends.*
- *Talking is the best way to solve a problem.*

17

PEER PRESSURE

UNDER PRESSURE OR IN CONTROL

Trying new things is all part of growing up, as is learning from your mistakes.

We usually know which new experiences come with a level of risk and if we decide to take that risk, hopefully we are doing so thoughtfully and carefully.

Some of the risky decisions we make in our teens can have a long-term affect on our lives. For example smoking; cigarettes are addictive—smoke one and it could mean a life sentence of smoking and ill-health—but, like everything, it is your choice and hopefully you are smart enough to make sensible decisions. However, there may be times when you feel under pressure to do something you don't want to do. Your friends might try to encourage you to do something that is not smart, or is just plain stupid. Hopefully you will have the confidence to stand up to them and say "no," but the pressure may get stronger and stronger. You may need to employ some different tactics if a simple "no" doesn't work, but ultimately, you'll feel better for having stood up for what you believe, rather than opting for an easy life and ending up in trouble, hurt, or hurting someone else.

"Some of my friends smoke. I hate it— and they know it!"

The simple rule is: if you feel unhappy or uncomfortable about doing something, then don't do it. If someone is forcing you to do something you feel unhappy about, perhaps it's time to ask yourself some questions about that particular friendship. Would a real friend put pressure on you to do something you didn't want to do? Would a real friend want to make you uncomfortable or unhappy?

ASK YOURSELF

HERE ARE SEVEN QUESTIONS TO ASK YOURSELF BEFORE MAKING ANY RISKY DECISION

- Is it dangerous or harmful?

- What are my instincts telling me?

- What have I got to lose?

- Do I feel under pressure?

- What are the potential consequences, to me, to my friends, to other people?

- Might any of my friends be thinking like me?

- What would my parents (or the closest person to me) think?

After thinking about the answers to these seven questions, do you still want to do it?

SO WHAT'S THE PROBLEM?

Do you think your friends are lame for not wanting to take risks? You're entitled to think that! The decisions you make for yourself are up to you—you wouldn't want to be told what to do, would you? So stop doing it to your friends. Respect their views and they'll respect yours.

Would a real friend want to cause you harm? It may seem a tough choice at the time but when you've made some new friends who respect your decisions, you'll realize that with the kind of friends who think nothing of putting you under unwanted pressure . . . you really don't need enemies!

"I just went along with it. I wish I hadn't."

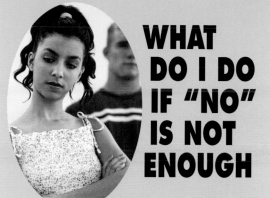

WHAT DO I DO IF "NO" IS NOT ENOUGH

If you're under pressure to do something you don't want to do, here are some ways to deal with it . . .

- **WALK AWAY FROM THE SITUATION**
  If your friends will not respect your decision or opinion, then you can just walk away and show "no" means no.

- **STAND YOUR GROUND**
  Saying no when everyone else is saying yes can make you feel left out, or worried about losing your friends. But you may actually find that if you stand your ground, others may be glad and fall in behind you.

- **SAY NO WITHOUT SAYING "NO"**
  Sometimes it is hard saying no to friends, especially if they don't see something as a big deal. So employ some clever get-out phrases like "You go ahead. I'll just stay here." "I would quite like to but it makes me feel sick." "I'm not really into this."

- **DECIDE IT'S TIME TO MAKE SOME NEW FRIENDS**
  If the pressure is making you uncomfortable, you need the safety net of other friends. It could be the best in the long run. Find friends who will respect your opinions and instincts.

OH NO, I'M A SMOKER

Sarah, 14, has become a smoker. What started out as just a way to shut friends up has now become a habit.

I started smoking when I was 13 and I really regret it. I basically just started because of these two friends of mine who were older than me. They were always smoking.

I was never interested, and I thought I was really strong. I'd always say no when they offered. But they kept on at me and then one day Ed said, "Just today, why don't you try one." I did it to shut them up and show them it just wasn't that big a deal. I hated it, but then the next time they asked I thought, "Well I'll just have one this time, because I had one before and it didn't do any harm." Then I had two. Then I couldn't keep bumming off them so I found myself scraping the money together to buy a pack. It was then I thought, "Oh my God, I'm a smoker," and I haven't stopped since.

> "I found myself scraping the money together to buy a pack."

ASK THE EXPERTS...

Simon the social worker says . . .
Peer pressure doesn't have to be a bad thing. It can be positive, too. You may even have done something good for a friend yourself! Like giving them advice, lending them something, or making someone laugh. So there's no reason some of your peers can't put some pressure on you to stop smoking if that's what you want. If you do want to stop you'll need all the help you can get.

Anita the counselor says . . .
Sadly, lots of people start smoking exactly the way you did so don't give yourself a hard time about it—nicotine is highly addictive. The good thing is that you aren't burying your head in the sand—you admit you have a problem. Quitting can be a challenge, so enlist the support of friends and your family if possible. The school nurse may be able to give you some tips.

Mac the family case worker says . . .
You obviously regret smoking, which is half-way to deciding to stop! Make yourself a list of pros and cons—what's good about smoking and what's bad. Add up how much money you've spent on cigarettes and what you will buy if you give up now. And next time friends suggest you do something you don't want to do, say no. If they're real friends, they'll understand and respect your decision.

I LET HER DOWN

Abby, 14, has got into shoplifting. Now she's worrying about the consequences.

"My sister said she didn't think I'd do anything that bad."

I got into shoplifting because a friend of mine named Cally did it and she made it seem like it was really funny and easy.

The first time we went shopping together she wanted me to do it with her. I said "I can't," and just walked away. When she came out of the shop afterward she made it seem so exciting, so I thought I'd have a go. It was a real buzz getting away with it. I was so nervous but felt so daring. After that, whenever we went out we'd steal. Then I began doing it on my own. My mom started questioning me about where I was getting all this stuff—she knows I don't have that much money. She asked my sister if I'd been stealing. My sister said she didn't think I'd do anything that bad, which made me feel really guilty. My mom got serious, saying how disappointed and upset they'd be if they thought I was doing something like that. I respect my mom—she's brought us up on her own—and it made me think about if the police got involved, how awful it would be for my mom. She's even said, "I trust you, Abby!" I've started making excuses to Cally and she's been really mean, saying I'm a mommy's girl and I'm pathetic. That's made me feel bad, too.

ASK THE EXPERTS...

Simon the social worker says . . . Peer pressure isn't the only pressure you have to cope with. There's also parent pressure! But having different people in our lives who give us different points of view is useful. It's handy to have a stock of different opinions on what's good and what's not. It's your decision though. Do you buy your friend's opinion that you're weak? Or take your mom's view that you're good?

Anita the counselor says . . . It isn't unusual for people to shoplift when they are still learning about the difference between right and wrong. Fortunately, you have had the sense to realize that it would affect your family as well as you if you were caught. Maybe Cally is jealous of the good relationship you have with your mom? Stick to friends who don't pressure you or make you feel bad.

Mac the family case worker says . . . There are ways of getting a buzz without shoplifting! Find more activities and interests so life becomes more exciting in a positive way. You obviously have a strong sense of responsibility and duty to your mom, which is good. Cally is not a good friend. Don't make excuses to her—tell her straight what you've been doing is wrong and you don't want to be a part of it anymore.

THEY'VE CALLED THE POLICE

Kieran, 13, was goofing around with his friends and they started a fire. Now the police have been called in.

My friends and I were just looking for something to do. Someone had the idea of breaking into our school. I don't think anyone intended to do it, we just were daring one another to see how far we would go.

We jumped the fence and ran across the field like commandos. It was funny! When we got to the school buildings, we were just goofing around—we'd split up into commando units and were trying to catch the others out. My friend, Will, went undercover by jumping into a garbage can where he found all these papers. I don't even

> "I'm terrified that one of my friends will tell someone."

know why now, but we thought it would be funny to set them alight. Will smokes so he had a lighter. As soon as he lit it, we realized it was a mistake, so we ran. Our other friends ran, too.

I didn't think anything until I heard on the local radio station that the police were appealing for information about a fire at the school. Not only had the can been damaged, but one of the school walls. I'm terrified that one of my friends will tell someone. I don't know what to do.

ASK THE EXPERTS . . .

Simon the social worker says . . . Sometimes when you are messing around with your friends, it is easy to get **carried away.** The trick when this happens is to realize what you have done and take a look at yourself. This incident has shaken you up, but you need to learn from it. Confess to your parents and a teacher, and accept the punishment. Hopefully this will convince you never to do anything like this again.

Anita the counselor says . . . When you get in with a group of tough friends, it is hard to say no. I can totally understand why you got involved in these pranks, but at least you know that you have done wrong. The best thing to do now is to put your hand up and admit to what has happened. People will think more of you for this, and you don't have to tell on any of your friends if you don't want to.

Mac the family case worker says . . . What a horrible situation for you to have got yourself **into.** I bet you feel pretty scared right now. The thing is, we all make mistakes when we are growing up. Tell your parents what has happened, and take their advice. If they tell you to own up, then so be it, but everyone will think more of you for having the courage to confess to this prank that went wrong.

THE OUTCOMES

After reading our experts' advice, Sarah, Abby, and Kieran wrote back to let us know how things turned out . . .

CASE STUDY 1

Don't kid yourself

I added it up and I've spent over $800 on cigarettes. What a waste. I don't even hang out with Ed and Jo anymore, but I do know Ed's stopped smoking. His new girlfriend told him he had to stop or she would dump him. I wish it were that easy for me. I do really want to give up. I know all the facts, like one cigarette takes five minutes of your life and stuff, but I'm still young and I don't want to live until I'm 100. But I will give up. I know I'll be able to if I want to.

CASE STUDY 2

Get back your pride

Cally and I drifted apart and now I'm glad because she's just got rougher and rougher. Her friends are bad news. Now when I think about what I did, I feel a bit sick. I wish I'd never done it. I'm glad I didn't let my mom down. I think maybe she knew what I was up to, but she gave me the opportunity to stop and get myself off the hook before anything really bad happened.

FOUL CIGARETTE FACTS

- Cigarettes contain formaldehyde—which is also used to preserve dead frogs.
- Nicotine, the ingredient in cigarettes that makes them addictive, is also used in some insect repellents.
- One drop of concentrated nicotine on the tongue will kill you!
- Just one cigarette contains a cocktail of 4,000 poisonous gases—at least 60 of which are known to cause cancer.

CASE STUDY 3

Think of the consequences

We did get caught. Someone had seen us jumping over the fence and he knew where one of my friends lived. It all came out then. I don't blame my friend for telling the police it was Will and I who'd started the fire. He was scared and I can't say I wouldn't have done the same thing. I was taken to the police station with my dad. The whole thing seemed familiar because I've seen so many police programs on TV, but this was happening to me. I had been arrested for arson! They put me inside this cell. I was in shock. It wasn't like we meant to damage anything. It was silly, stupid, beyond dumb. I was interviewed for ages. My dad was in the room, too, but I couldn't look at him. I was so terrified that I just wanted to cry. In the end I got a warning, which means I've got a criminal record. My parents might have to pay for some of the damage, too. Mom's been all right but Dad was angry, really angry.

MISFIT CITY

HOW DO YOU FIT IN?

School presents many opportunities to form strong friendships and become part of a group. But what about those who have problems fitting in or who are seen by others as an outsider?

School is "clique heaven." Being in a clique gives you confidence and makes you feel safe, but without a clique you could be thought of as a misfit—worse still, you could feel like one. It can feel tough if you don't seem to be able to find a niche to fit you.

"I've got the best friends ever!"

A big part of being who you are has to do with how you project yourself to the outside world. Virtually everything you do, say, or wear says something about how you see yourself. It can be difficult to express yourself when you feel overly aware of other people looking at you or judging you. But remember, if you feel confident about yourself (even if it's just a front to begin with) it's more likely that people will accept you as you are.

It's in us all—this desire to be part of something. In school, we want to be part of a group of friends, or to have a group to hang around and have fun with. But what if you're on the outside trying to get in, or on the inside being pushed out? What are you supposed to do then? What if you have tried everything to feel like an accepted member of a group but still they treat you as an outsider?

The answer is to walk away. It's important to keep your self-respect and not allow others to treat you badly. But it takes bravery—you might worry or be scared that you'll have no friends, but if people are being mean to you, they're not real friends so you have nothing to lose. Set yourself free and you'll be open to new people and new groups of friends who will value you so much more. And if you find yourself in a crowd that treats others who don't fit in with scorn or even bullies them, you need to have a long, hard think. Are you really comfortable with it? Do you feel that person deserves to be treated that way? If the answer's no, then be brave, because you might find yourself outside of a clique one day, hoping someone will give you a break.

"They don't include me anymore. I'm being pushed out."

CELEBRITY MISFITS

Many celebrities have suffered at the hands of bullies. They have all gone on to be far more successful than their bullies could even imagine!

- **EMINEM— RAPPER**
  Eminem was always the "new kid" because he changed schools so much. Because of this he was subjected to bullying and one violent attack, which he wrote about in his song "Brain Damage."

- **TOM CRUISE— HOLLYWOOD FILM STAR**
  Tom Cruise is dyslexic and because of this he was teased at school. "My childhood was extremely lonely. I was dyslexic and lots of kids made fun of me. That experience made me tough inside, because you learn to quietly accept "

- **KATE WINSLET— HOLLYWOOD FILM STAR**
  The star of Titanic was a chubby teenager and was a victim of torments. "At 16 I was 182 pounds, and was nicknamed 'blubber.' It was pathetic and childish, but girls can be so catty . . . Eventually I must have told my mother, and she took it up with the teachers. They dealt with the situation without exposing my identity."

THE ODD ONE OUT

Rob, 14, did not have friends of his own when he started high school. He tagged along with others, but always felt like the odd one out.

> "They made fun of me all the time. I'd just have to take it because I didn't really have any other friends."

I had a year when we all went on to high school where I just always seemed to be on my own. Most of my friends had gone to another school and I only knew two boys from my old school, Jake and Cameron, so I tagged along with them.

They were already quite good friends and I was the odd one out. They'd do mean things like get me to go to the stores and when I'd get back they'd be gone. And they made fun of me all the time. I'd just have to take it because I didn't really have any other friends. They'd pick on me and start fights, saying things like, "We don't want to hang out with you anymore, you're too wimpy." I'd pretend I didn't care but I really hated the fact that everyone else seemed to have good friends and I was always the odd one out. It's much harder than it was at elementary school. There you could just walk up and start talking to another kid. You can't really do that now.

ASK THE EXPERTS...

Simon the social worker says . . .
Leaving elementary school often means losing friends. Going to high school means getting used to new people, places, and subjects. And it means making new friends, too. It can take a while to find your feet again. In the meantime, there's nothing wrong with taking second best. But keep an eye out for true friendship.

Anita the counselor says . . .
You had lots of friends at elementary school so the chances are that you will have a wider circle of friends again. Use this experience to make sure that you aren't unpleasant to anyone less popular than yourself! You say that it's harder just to walk up to people at high school, do you have hobbies or interests that might bring you into a wider social group?

Mac the family case worker says . . .
It's a hard time when you change schools. Obviously Cameron and Jake were not suitable friends, and at some point will learn a hard lesson if they continue to enjoy being unpleasant. If you want to make good friends, start by being a good listener. Everyone values someone who is sympathetic and supportive. Be kind to others, and you'll soon find everyone values you and wants your company.

THEY'RE DOING MY HEAD IN

Ben, 13, is finding it difficult dividing his time between two groups of friends who hate each other.

I've got two groups of friends—one group that I go around with mostly at school and then another group who I go into town with more on weekends.

Some people in the two groups really hate each other and they are always ragging on each other. When they say horrible things about someone I like I just say, "He's alright." But I'm so bored of their feuding and them giving me a hard time about being friends with the others. It's not as if they're any different or anything. I don't think they even know why they don't like each other anymore.

> "It's not as if they're any different or anything."

ASK THE EXPERTS...

Simon the social worker says . . .
You are stuck in the middle between people who hate each other.
You might believe you could help them sort it out. But nobody's asking you to help. What they want is to complain about each other. Let each group know you enjoy spending time with them. Tell them you don't want to hear these problems. Suggest they talk to each other directly.

Anita the counselor says . . .
It's good to hear that you are popular enough to hang out with two different groups of friends. I'm also glad to hear that you don't join in with back stabbing. You sound more mature than some of your friends who are just looking for the differences between them—you recognize that they have things in common. Use your social skills to pick friends who are mature enough not to be possessive.

Mac the family case worker says . . .
You need to have some ready-made responses or this will wear you out!
Think of things you want to say and practice them, like "I don't want to hear you making fun of my friends" or "If you two have a problem, talk to each other about it and leave me out. It's boring!" Perhaps it's time to join some new clubs and activities so you can make friends with people who are ready to enjoy themselves, not spend their time moaning!

SHE'S A LIAR

Michaela, 15, is frustrated because another girl is trying to muscle in on her group of friends. She won't leave Michaela alone.

There's this girl in my class, Claire, who's really annoying. She's always sucking up to me and my friends, saying she likes our clothes, our hair, etc., even if we're wearing our school uniform! She wants to be one of us, but she'll never be because she's a creep and none of us like her.

She keeps sending me text messages, asking what we're doing and where we're going. Anyway, I started calling her this name and then all my friends started calling her it, too. She asked me why I was being so mean and I told her honestly—"I don't like you. Leave us alone!" but she just went running straight to the teacher and started crying. Now I've been accused of bullying and my teacher has said she will send a letter home if there's any more of it. Now Claire's feeling all confident. She's still trying to hang around with us, but she says I can't be mean to her anymore or she'll tell on me. Why won't she just leave us alone and find her own friends?

> "She wants to be one of us, but she'll never be because she's a creep."

ASK THE EXPERTS...

Simon the social worker says . . . Your classmate has a lot going for her! She's obviously smart and assertive, not to mention having good taste! There may come a time when you want someone like that on your side. Calling her names didn't get rid of her. She used your verbal bullying against you. And now she's pushed her way into your group. So why not relax. Be kinder to her. Introduce her to everyone you know. She may relax, too, and make more friends.

Anita the counselor says . . . There will always be people who you have to deal with but don't like. It can be very annoying when people latch on to you and this has obviously provoked you into some pretty strong behavior. If you really couldn't find it in your heart to allow Claire into your group, maybe you could have politely told her she wasn't welcome and avoided the unpleasant consequences of being accused of bullying.

Mac the family case worker says . . . You were unkind to call Claire names. She may be clingy and irritating, but she obviously has problems making friends. Try being civil without being friendly. It sounds as if you are a leader and your group looks up to you. Set them a good example and try to be a little more sympathetic to Claire. When things have died down, you can explain why you were so irritated by her to your teacher and can ask for help.

THE OUTCOMES

After reading our experts' advice, Rob, Ben, and Michaela wrote back to let us know how things turned out . . .

GET CONNECTED

American Counseling Association
5999 Stevenson Avenue
Alexandria, VA 22304

CASE STUDY 1

It's not forever

I've got quite a good circle of friends now. One break, these other boys were playing a game I am really good at. I started giving them tips on how to play and we just started hanging out after that. It was really weird because Jake and Cameron started being all friendly toward me again but then I thought, "No, get lost, you weren't interested before, so why should you be now?" But I suppose I'm just as bad. If a new kid starts, there's no way I'd be the first one to talk to them or be friendly, it's just not cool . . . I guess I'm just glad it's not me!

CASE STUDY 2

Move on

I got so fed up with it I just found some other friends who weren't into the group thing. I've stayed friendly with most of them, but this one guy takes his gang really seriously and said if I'm out, I'm out. Like it bothers me! My new friends and I just have a laugh and that's how I like it. I don't need grief from my friends.

CASE STUDY 3

Life isn't always fair

Claire really pushed it one day. She was grabbing me and being even more annoying than I thought she was capable of, so I hit her. I knew I shouldn't have but she shouldn't have touched me. I got into real trouble.

I was given detention and my parents grounded me. Now when my friends go into town, they have to put up with her tagging along or they'll get into trouble, too. So I'm the one stuck at home and Claire's out with my friends. It's not fair.

REMEMBER

• Being part of a group can be reassuring and fun, but it can also have its problems. Don't get locked in to one group of friends.
• Don't ever hang around with people who are mean to you.
• If you are in a group, don't be mean to others—you don't know who you may need on your side in the future.

BULLY BOYS . . . AND GIRLS

BULLYING IS DAMAGING

Bullying can take many forms—the most extreme form is physical abuse, but verbal abuse can be equally as hurtful and damaging. And then there is being ignored or teased, milder maybe but they can affect your self-esteem and turn your school days into a nightmare if it isn't stopped. Bullying is cruel and no one deserves it.

Racism is a form of bullying or abuse where people make judgements about others based on the color of their skin. It is completely irrational and those with prejudices are usually poorly informed. It is their own fear of anything "different" that prompts this kind of attitude—but merely reflects their own insecurities.

WHY DO PEOPLE BULLY?

PEOPLE BULLY OTHERS FOR A VARIETY OF REASONS. HERE ARE SOME . . .

- They are or have been bullied themselves
- They are angry or frustrated and take it out on others
- They don't have friends
- They have problems at home
- They are insecure and want to feel "big"
- They are egged on by friends
- They are selfish or spoiled
- They want to be in control
- They are aggressive and don't think about others feelings
- They like the feeling of having power over others

"They find it fun. I don't know what to do."

BUT WHY ME?

It could be any number of reasons—from wearing glasses, to being clever. Bullies need a victim. If you're sensitive, they know they can press buttons to make you react. If you're not used to conflict, they enjoy watching you squirm and know you won't fight back. Don't allow yourself to be victimized. You don't deserve it.

There's no real thought behind a bully's behavior and once people start standing up to them, they are unlikely to back up their opinions with any reasonable argument.

So how do you stop bullying? Well, first, stand up for yourself, even if you feel terrified inside. If you show the bully that they aren't getting to you, they'll soon get bored and leave you alone. It can be hard, but you need to try to be confident in yourself. If you have tried everything, your school is there to help and support you. Hopefully they will have an anti-bullying policy in place and will have a clear set of guidelines on how to deal with bullying. If they don't have such a policy, you might be the catalyst required to organize them on that front!

But sometimes bullying takes place outside of the school grounds—at bus stops, in town, or on the train. Again, there are ways to deal with it other than trying to stand up for yourself possibly against people older and more aggressive than you. Just don't suffer in silence. The only way to stop it is to talk to an adult you know will help you sort it out. You may worry that it is going to make things worse, but in the long run it will mean that you get the support you need to deal with the problem. Never let it get so bad that you want to skip school or stay at home. You owe it to yourself not to let that happen.

BEAT THE BULLY

Here are some tips on dealing with bullies:

- **WALK AWAY** *It's tricky to keep bullying someone who won't stay around to listen.*

- **DON'T FIGHT BACK** *You'll probably end up making the situation worse. It's not worth it.*

- **BE PREPARED** *If you know there's a certain thing about you that the bully usually attacks, have a reply ready.*

- **AVOID THE SITUATION** *If there's a place where the bully usually corners you, avoid it.*

- **HANG OUT WITH A GROUP** *Try not to be on your own too much. Bullies like to pick on people who have no back-up.*

- **LOOK ASSERTIVE** *If you act confident (even if you're not) people often believe what they see.*

- **KEEP A RECORD** *If you're constantly being picked on, keep a diary of it. It will make it easier to prove what's been happening.*

- **TAKE CONTROL** *Do something to build or maintain your self-esteem—join a karate club or gym. It's not about fighting back, it's about having the physical confidence as well as mental strength.*

- **TELL SOMEONE** *Most important of all, tell someone what is going on. It could be parents, a teacher, a friend, or phone a help line—they're all there to support you.*

HE'S SO SCARY

Owen, 12, and his friends are feeling intimidated by the school bully. They want to stand up to him but then again, they don't want to get beaten up!

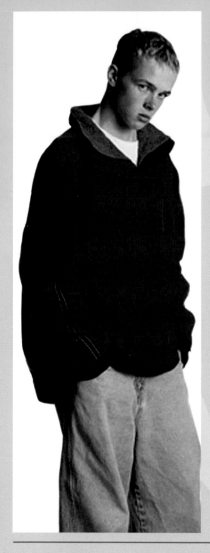

There is this boy named Tom who has a real reputation for being scary. He's so unpredictable —he'll have you as a friend one minute and then if you say something wrong he immediately turns against you.

He gets really angry over nothing and shouts in your face. He pushed a friend of mine down some steps the other day. When my friend pointed out that Tom could have really hurt him, he just said, "I wish you HAD fallen." Then, to cover himself, he told a teacher that my friend had hit him for no reason. It was a pack of lies. My friends want to stand up to him. We say "Okay, today's the day. We'll do it together," but then he says something and we just back off, worried that he'll pound us! But now a new boy's come to the school. Alex is just really, really strong— he isn't scared of anything. Tom tried to bully him, but Alex didn't even flinch. You can tell Tom doesn't know what to do.

> "He gets really angry over nothing and shouts in your face."

ASK THE EXPERTS...

Simon the social worker says . . .
Some people like to have power over other people. They enjoy being able to do what they like. They're a school problem, not just your problem. Having friends who support each other against bullies like these is a big plus. But there's no need to stand up to him. Together you can decide to completely ignore him.

Anita the counselor says . . .
Tom's obviously got problems since he's unpredictable and overreacts to things. It sounds like sticking together could be the answer in standing up to him. Alex has given an example of what can happen when Tom's reputation doesn't impress—he's stood up to him and lived to tell the tale. Changing your behavior as a group could make him think twice before trying to bully you.

Mac the family case worker says . . .
Bullies are cowards underneath. Lying to a teacher showed that Tom is being very manipulative. With Alex's help, if you all support each other, bullies like Tom won't have a chance. The problem of bullying won't go away if you just ignore it. Tell a trusted adult if you are being bullied. Keep telling until something is done. You have a right to feel safe.

I COULDN'T TELL MY MOM

Charmaine, now 16, was bullied by a girl—the daughter of her mom's best friend.

From about 11 I was really bullied. She'd say stuff like, "Fatty, better get some liposuction."

The girl, Mandy, was the daughter of my mom's best friend. That's why I kept quiet about it for so long, because they were so close. Mandy was in the year above me. When I started high school, she just went for me. It was weird because Mandy had been bullied and my big sister, Jenna,

> "When I started high school, she just went for me."

had stuck up for her, but that didn't make any difference. It mostly happened on the school bus in front of everybody. No one stood up for me or said anything.

Then one day, she got my hairbrush out of my schoolbag and was hitting me with it. I just couldn't take it anymore. I went to my teacher and he said he'd talk to her. Next thing I knew he'd called me back saying that Mandy was "deeply upset" and couldn't believe I'd accuse her of such a thing. She told him our families were friends and how close we were. He said that if I ever accuse her again, he'd make sure I didn't go back to the school. He was just so horrible.

ASK THE EXPERTS...

Simon the social worker says . . .
Your parents need to approach the principal about the teacher's comments, since these were unacceptable. No one could "make sure you don't go back to school" on such flimsy evidence. However, just because one person handled it badly, don't stop "telling" when you have a problem. Keep trying until you find someone who WILL listen!

Anita the counselor says . . .
It's really unfortunate when people you trust misunderstand you. Mandy sounds manipulative and she seems to be trying to transfer her problems on to you. It was kind of you to try to protect your mom's friendship, but I'm sure your mom would be happier protecting you in the circumstances! Tell your mom all about it, or if you prefer, ask Jenna to get involved on your behalf to explain what has been going on.

Mac the family case worker says . . .
No one deserves to be bullied. It is the responsibility of all those in authority to listen and to help you feel safe. The first thing you must do is tell somebody. Tell your mom, tell your sister Jenna, and get somebody to confront your teacher about their attitude to bullying. If they won't listen, tell your mom to arrange a meeting with the principal, who should be able to sort this situation out for you.

• BULLY BOYS . . . AND GIRLS •

THERE'S NO ESCAPE

Carly, now 15, remembers last year as a really miserable time because of a girl who was making her life hell.

> "I was really anxious and upset all the time. I didn't want to leave the house."

Last year this tough girl was really making my life miserable. She and her family moved in behind my house and she just had a go at me right from the start. She'd start mouthing off as soon as she saw me in the morning and then all the way to school, saying horrible racist things.

She'd even say horrible things about my mom because Mom's blonde and my brothers are white. I was really anxious and upset all the time. I didn't want to leave the house and I used to get rides to school and back because I didn't want to walk. But she was like that at school, too, so it felt like there was

no escape. Then the police got involved because my mom contacted them and the girl and her family moved away. I was so much happier— for a few days. Another family moved in and the woman used to wear American flag stuff and say things about, "going back to my own country." My mom got in touch with the police again, but they didn't really do much, so she got in touch with the public housing council and this time they moved us and everything's been okay since.

ASK THE EXPERTS...

Simon the social worker says . . .
Racist behavior is unacceptable and it's against the law. You shouldn't have to deal with it on your own. If someone is racist toward you tell an adult who you trust. Support from the police, your school, and the local government can help. It's their job to sort it out. But your family and friends will understand what you're going through better. And it's at times like these that we find out just how important they are.

Anita the counselor says . . .
It sounds like you've had a really hard time having to go through such a bad experience with neighbors twice. Your mom has shown you a great example though, in standing up to these racist bullies and not accepting their behavior. I hope that will have taught you to have confidence in yourself and to speak up for yourself when you need to.

Mac the family case worker says . . .
Be proud of who you are. You may not look like your brothers and mom, but you could be very like them in character! A bully will find any excuse to pick on a victim—it could be race, height, hair color, interests. Be true to yourself. Real friends will like you for who you are. Your mom is obviously capable of handling these bullies in a very effective way. Talk to her about how you feel.

THE OUTCOMES

After reading our experts' advice, Owen, Charmaine, and Carly wrote back to let us know how things turned out . . .

GET CONNECTED

American Psychological Association
750 First Street, NE
Washington, D.C. 20002

CASE STUDY 1

Bullies can be beaten

Alex really knocked Tom off his pedestal. When everyone saw that he could be beaten, Tom just wasn't as scary anymore. Luckily Alex is a really nice guy and on the whole things have calmed right down. Tom tries to be a bully sometimes, but no one really takes him seriously any more.

CASE STUDY 2

It helps to talk

When my mom finally realized what was going on she phoned the principal. He said he had never been made aware of it—so my teacher hadn't even bothered telling him. We were always getting lectures in health class about bullying and how the school wouldn't tolerate it—it just made me want to scream. My mom knew how bad it was and so set up a meeting with me, the bully, and her mom. It was awful because up to that point, I'd felt like everyone was ganging up on me, no one would believe me. Our families have sort of fallen out. Her mom did apologize to me, so I think Mandy admitted it in the end, but that doesn't make up for anything. In one way, though, I think she did me a favor. She really made me want to lose weight and I did. And the more weight I lost, the more confident I became. So that now I don't even think I'd be the sort of person that would put up with that sort of thing anymore.

CASE STUDY 3

Things will get better

That year did change me. At the time I really lost confidence and I felt really shy and vulnerable. But afterward I felt stronger, because I just thought that's it, I don't care what anybody else thinks or says about me, I know I'm okay. Whenever somebody says something racist or horrible about my family now, I always call them out on it right away, telling them how stupid they are being. Normally they are so embarrassed about being confronted in this way that they don't bother me again.

REMEMBER

- You don't deserve to be bullied.
- There are many people who can help you, so don't stop until you get the help you need.
- It's the bully who has the problem. Don't allow them to victimize you.
- Talk to someone. It will help.

OH NO . . . I'M IN TROUBLE

CLASS CLASHES
OR SERIOUS SCRAPES

Every school has its own rules and expected standards of behavior. Step over the line and your messing with the school's authority. And you are going to pay!

Not everybody can make it through school without getting in trouble at some time. It may be that you just made a bad decision at some point, or that you wanted attention, or that you have a serious ax to grind with authority. Whatever the reasons, going against the school system is always going to be a "no-win" situation.

Aside from their aims of educating you to an accepted standard, schools also endeavor to turn you into good citizens. That means being respectful and considerate of others, and accepting the laws of the land. Being rude to your teachers, bullying your classmates, or breaking the school rules shows them that you aren't quite mastering the principles of good citizenship and so it leads to one thing—discipline! It's the only thing the school has in its power and it's not afraid to use it.

"The school rules are so petty."

"I'm glad we can't bring cell phones in to school. Mine's embarrassing!"

Schools differ. Some have a relaxed, flexible attitude, others could feel like boot camp, but most schools fall somewhere in between. What they have in common is that they all have rules and their own ways of dealing with those who break them.

Schools are too big and busy to really reflect on the reasons why one student might be giving cause for concern. Everyone's bad behavior is met with the same response—whether that is detention for a mild offense or expulsion for a major one. If you've got problems, it's generally more productive to actually come out with it and talk to someone—a far better way of getting understanding or help than misbehaving in the hope that someone might actually notice you. Don't jump to the conclusion that teachers don't care if they don't know a problem exists. Teachers, support staff, school counselors, and family case workers are all there to help. And remember, just because you've messed up on more than one occasion, it doesn't mean you're a bad seed headed for a life of crime. Even the most badly behaved kids can turn into successful and respected professionals proving everybody wrong.

DOES YOUR ATTITUDE STINK?
TAKE THIS TEST TO FIND OUT...

1. **Your teacher yells at you for something that isn't your fault. Do you . . .**
a) Angrily protest and be as rude as you like?
B) Get your mom to call the principal?
C) Protest and tell him how it really happened?
D) Look at him open-mouthed but decide to talk to him later about it?

2. **You're wearing something that is against the school rules. Why?**
a) It's a petty, stupid rule and you'll wear what you like.
B) Your mom said you could.
C) You've got a good reason. You thought it would be okay, just this once.
D) You just forgot.

3. **You're struggling to understand what your teacher is trying to teach you. What do you do?**
a) Nothing. It's boring and you couldn't care less whether you understand it or not.
B) Nothing. She's just a bad teacher.
C) You ask her to go over it again.
D) You wait till class is over and then ask her for help.

4. **You're really late for school. What are you thinking?**
a) It's no big deal. What are they going to do about it?
B) It was the bus driver's fault. He could see you running.
C) Oops, but at least you'll miss homeroom.
D) You'd better hurry or you'll get into trouble.

MOSTLY AS – Yes, your attitude stinks and you know it. You might even be proud of it. But you're not doing yourself any favors. No diploma and a "couldn't care less" attitude is not going to get you a well-paid job when you leave school. Maybe you don't care about that either, but think about the kind of life you want in the future and what you need to do to achieve it. Wise up, for your own sake.

MOSTLY BS – It's never your fault, is it? You don't want to take responsibility for anything. Hopefully your attitude will change when you become a bit more mature. You'll realize that once you start taking responsibility, you will feel more self-assured and in control of your life.

MOSTLY CS – Your attitude to school and life in general is fairly figured out. You don't take it all too seriously. You push it sometimes to see what you can get away with, but on the whole you're respectful, smart, and mature.

MOSTLY DS – You care about school and you care about your future. You want to do well and are clever enough to realize that a good education is going to help you achieve your aims.

DETENTION, DETENTION

Chris, 14, has little respect for one of his teachers who is always giving him detention.

I'm always getting detention from this one teacher. It's not just me—she gives detention over nothing. I think it's the only thing she can think of to make us do what she wants us to do.

There's lunchtime detention if you haven't done work and then there's detention after school, where you have to clean up and do chores around the school. She'll give out detention over anything—talking, throwing stuff, answering her back. And it's a complete waste of time, it doesn't stop me from doing it again. I don't know why she's a teacher if she hates kids so much. She should get herself a nice office job and do us all a favor.

> "I don't know why she's a teacher if she hates kids so much."

ASK THE EXPERTS...

Simon the social worker says . . . It sounds like your teacher isn't the only one who's stuck in a rut. There she is giving detention after detention never changing what she does. And there you are getting detention after detention never changing what you do! Surprise her by doing something different. Be helpful. Ask for advice about a problem. Talk about your interests.

Anita the counselor says . . . Unfortunately we all meet individuals in life that are not as supportive and helpful as we would like. Maybe this teacher thinks she's doing you a favor in focusing you on your work! It sounds as though most of the time that's being wasted is yours though. Surely there are things you'd rather be doing than detention? Rise to the challenge of escaping her attention and get a life!

Mac the family case worker says . . . Do you expect this teacher to reward you for answering her back? Perhaps she's frustrated because there are children in your class who want to learn, and you are stopping them. Give the woman a break. Meet her halfway. You may find she has something interesting to teach you! If she really is picking on you when you've made an effort, ask your parents to discuss the problem with your principal.

WHAT'S THE POINT?

Dan, 14, became disillusioned after his parents split up. He drifted in to a different crowd.

My mom and dad split up and, I know it's a bit cliché, but I went on the wrong path for a bit. I was really upset but I felt like no one cared. The school was useless—my teacher knew about it and she was really embarrassed when she offered me support.

Everything seemed pointless—what was the point of studying and getting a good education when it couldn't keep your parents together? Why was I trying to make them proud anyway?

> "What was the point of studying and getting a good education when it couldn't keep your parents together?"

I started hanging out with these boys that had a reputation for being a bit wild—they weren't really that bad, a lot of it was just a front, but they were always getting in trouble for vandalism and smoking. I just drifted into it, too. Before I had been good at school—behavior and grades and everything—and it all started slipping. Mom and Dad were always being called in and now, looking back, I guess it was one way I could be sure of getting them in a room together! I think I was just really miserable and vandalizing stuff was a rush for a bit. Smoking with them made me feel part of something.

ASK THE EXPERTS...

Simon the social worker says . . . People do all sorts of things to make themselves feel better. Homework isn't everyone's first choice. Often it's something risky, like smoking or drinking. It gives you a high but it also harms you. Think what would give you a safer and legal buzz. Ask yourself what you used to enjoy. Find out what your old friends are into now. Ask your parents to support you in a new interest.

Anita the counselor says . . . You've been through a difficult time with your parents splitting up. It sounds as if you've got a good track record academically and that sticks just as much as having had a period of acting up. You show some insight into your need to feel a part of something. Hopefully you will make some sensible judgements when life has settled down with your parents living apart and you realize that they both still care about you.

Mac the family case worker says . . . It's very painful when parents break up and you feel like you're in the middle. You need to remember that you have your own life. Your parents still love you and care for you even if they're not together. Choose friends who can share more positive interests. Showing your parents you are making a success of your life is the best way to keep them close to you.

I CAN'T STAND MY TEACHER

Kylie, 14, has a teacher who she thinks is inconsiderate. She stands up to him and is always getting into trouble.

My Geography teacher is really horrible and I can't stand him. It's summer and he won't even let me open a window. The classroom smells so bad, but he just shouts at me because I'm interrupting his lesson. My friends and I think he wants the windows shut because it makes the room so hot that all the girls have to strip.

Everybody else just puts up with him, but I'm not like that. Yes, he's a teacher and I'm supposed to do what he says, but don't ask me to respect him. He should earn my respect like everyone else. I mean, I only wanted to open a window and I got detention!

I see him leaning over girls, looking down their tops. He does it to me and I tell him where to go. Then I'm in detention again, or get sent to the principal. I can't win. What can I do about it? Why should I have to put up with him just because I'm a kid?

> "Why should I have to put up with him just because I'm a kid?"

ASK THE EXPERTS...

Simon the social worker says . . .
You could try approaching this teacher in a less confrontational way so he has less reason to refuse a reasonable request! Ask him before the lesson starts if you could open the window because it's stuffy and you find it difficult to concentrate in the heat. Respect works both ways—you say he needs to "earn" your respect—perhaps you need to think about how to earn his, too!

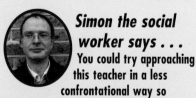

Anita the counselor says . . .
If you really think his behavior is uncomfortable, tell your parents, and make an appointment to have a private meeting with the principal to discuss your worries. Remember that people will be more inclined to take your comments seriously if you don't confuse the issue by being unnecessarily confrontational about it. There are ways in which you can state your complaint without being rude or disruptive.

Mac the family case worker says . . .
I remember when I was at school there were lots of teachers I didn't like. You need to figure out whether you just don't like this man or if he really is a bit of a **pervert**. If he is crossing the line with you or any of the other girls, you must tell somebody such as your mom or dad or another teacher. You should never have to put up with this sort of behavior however old you are.

THE OUTCOMES

After reading our experts' advice, Chris, Dan, and Kylie told us how things turned out . . .

GET CONNECTED

**Parents Without Partners
401 North Michigan Avenue
Chicago, IL 60611**

PWP is an international organization that provides help for people facing parenthood after being divorced, separated, or widowed.

C A S E   S T U D Y   1

It's up to you

Getting detention started getting to be a real drag because I missed out on what my friends were doing. **They started meeting up with these girls on the bus and I was stuck in detention.** So I started getting really angry but that just got me into worse trouble. I had to go to the teacher who gave me even more detention and said if it carried on he'd put it on my permanent record. I'm trying to curb it. I haven't changed the way I think about this teacher, but I'm not going to let her spoil my fun.

C A S E   S T U D Y   2

Put it behind you

As time went by, I think I got used to my new life with Mom and Dad living separately, because they were still supportive and I knew they still cared about me. And I got bored with the other group. They were pretty dumb really, which is why they were into vandalizing stuff—they didn't think they were ever going to make anything of their lives. But I'm not stupid and after a while I got bored with doing the same old stuff, making the same old jokes, making fun of people in a way that was totally not funny. I just drifted away from them and back to some of my old friends. The school seems to have brushed it under the carpet, too —no one talks about it, which suits me fine! Before everyone did nothing but talk and I was so bored by it I didn't want to listen.

C A S E   S T U D Y   3

There's always a way

The principal realized that there was what he called "a clash of personalities." He asked my mom to go in and they all talked about it together. I wanted to be included but they wouldn't let me, which I thought was so typical! Anyway, the upside was that I changed classes. It was a pain because it also meant that I had to juggle my whole schedule and couldn't stay in the same French class either. That was a drag because I really liked that teacher, but it all worked out okay. I'm glad I got away from him and wasn't getting into so much trouble.

MOVING ON

At school end

It may seem like a lifetime away, but you will leave school one day and it's not too early to focus on your end goal.

When you get to 14, you need to start making some decisions about your education and what you want to do when your school days finally come to an end.

Soon, you're going to be at a crossroads. It forces you to focus on what you want to do after school. Do you want to go to college? Is there a particular job or career you'd like to pursue? If so, what qualifications will you need?

> "I did work experience recently. I really enjoyed it but it was really like working life."

It's important to consider what you are personally interested in as well as what you are good at when making decisions about your future—it's not what your mom and dad want you to do, or even what your friends are doing that counts most. But, that said, be prepared to take advice—after all there are many people out there with a lot of life experiences they might be willing to share. And if you decide to take the simplest option of choosing things you find easy or fun, maybe you should think a bit harder. The easy option isn't always the best. Choosing school subjects seems like a big decision, but you're not closing any doors that you can't reopen later.

BE WHAT YOU WANT TO BE

TO ACHIEVE YOUR GOALS, WHATEVER THEY MAY BE, YOU GENERALLY NEED SOME, IF NOT ALL OF THE FOLLOWING . . .

- Enthusiasm – **be passionate about it**

- Self-motivation – **keep going and you'll get there**

- Focus – **don't lose sight of the end goal**

- Good communication skills – **talk, listen, and learn**

- An interest in people – **getting others on your side can help and you can learn from others' experiences**

- Self-discipline – **be strict with yourself**

- Education – **knowledge is power**

If you drop History or Biology and find out you need it to get in a course later on down the line, you can always pick it up again at a college. It might delay you and it might mean missed opportunities, but at least you've found something you know you want to do and have a sense of purpose rather than drifting from one thing to another without finding anything that really grabs you. If, however, you've identified a particular career or job you would love, try to get involved on a voluntary basis. You may find out you love it, or that it's not for you after all . . . which is great, because it's much easier to change your mind about something before you begin, rather than half-way through.

And if all this is sounding far too serious, maybe you'll decide to take a year off after school to travel, or to work before college to earn lots of money. Don't get hung up about the future—you just need to think about it. Set your sights on what you want and put some thought into how you're going to get there. Then go for it . . . and have a great life!

HAVE A PLAN

If you don't know what you want to do, here's an exercise to make you think.

Write down three jobs you might like to do. Why are you drawn to those jobs? Is it because . . .

a) *You'll earn good money?*
B) *You'll be looked up to and respected?*
C) *It's an interesting job?*
D) *It will suit your skills and the lifestyle you want?*
e) *You think you would be good at it?*
F) *It's always what you've wanted to do?*
G) *It's something your parents/teacher/ guidance counselor has suggested to you?*
H) *One of your parents does it?*
I) *Someone you know does it and likes it?*
J) *It sounds good?*
K) *You don't know why?*

If you answered yes to any or all of questions (A) to (E), it shows that you are giving your future some kind of careful consideration. If you answered yes to (F) or (G), then you might want to think whether it is really right for you. If you answered yes to any or all of questions (H) to (K), then it seems that you are a long way off from setting some career goals. There are thousands of different jobs, so why not look into those within an area that interests you.

WHAT ARE YOU GOOD AT?

Test yourself to discover your strengths and weaknesses—
if you know those, you'll soon be on the path to success.

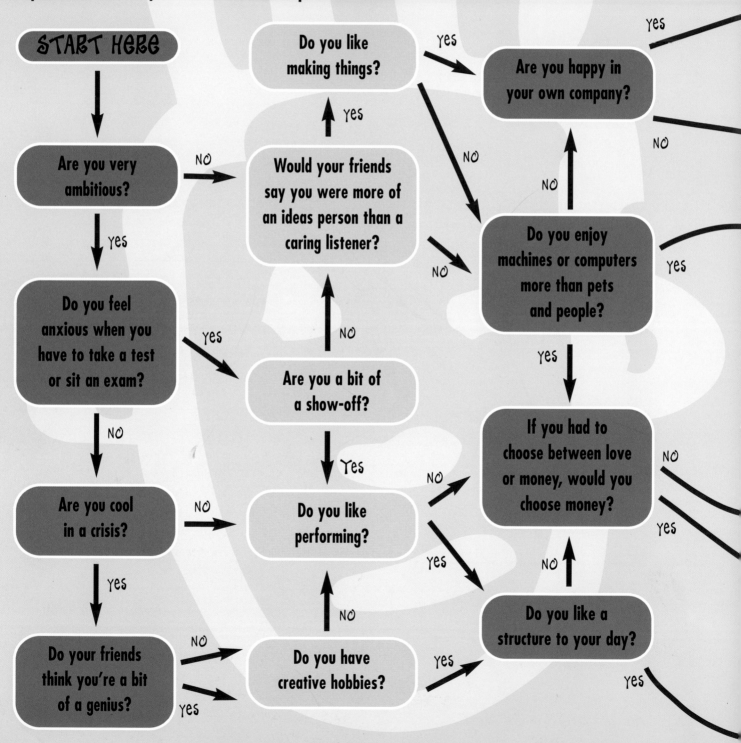

START HERE

Are you very ambitious? — NO →

↓ YES

Do you feel anxious when you have to take a test or sit an exam? — YES →

↓ NO

Are you cool in a crisis? — NO →

↓ YES

Do your friends think you're a bit of a genius? — NO →

↓ YES

Do you like making things? — YES →

↑ YES

Would your friends say you were more of an ideas person than a caring listener? — NO →

↓ NO

Are you a bit of a show-off?

↓ Yes

Do you like performing? — NO →

↑ NO

Do you have creative hobbies? — YES →

Are you happy in your own company? YES / NO

↑ NO

Do you enjoy machines or computers more than pets and people?

↓ YES

If you had to choose between love or money, would you choose money? NO / YES

↑ NO

Do you like a structure to your day? — YES

44

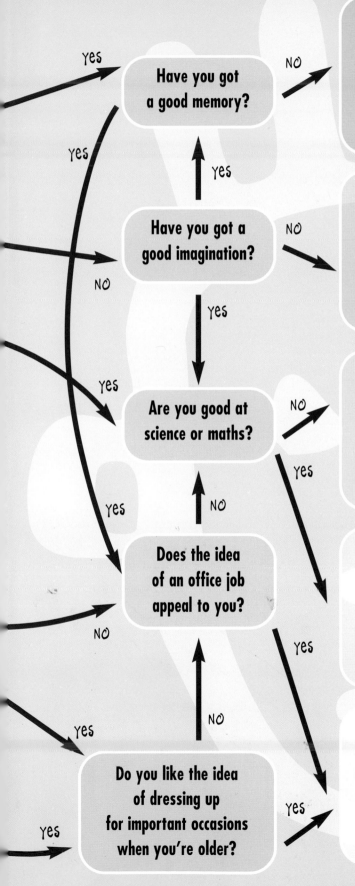

ARTISTIC

You're a creative type, always trying something new. Make the most of your artistic flair but don't limit yourself to the obvious options. There are so many careers in the arts apart from artist and designer.

CARING

You're calm in a crisis, a good listener, and as patient as the day is long. You work well as part of a team and could be heading for a career with a caring side where money isn't the most important thing.

DRAMA QUEEN/KING

You're strength is being able to stand out in a crowd. Your name could be in lights one day, but even the most talented of performers underpin their talent with a sound knowledge of literature, music, or the arts.

PRACTICAL

You're a real problem-solver—good in a crisis. You enjoy working alone, but are not someone who would be happy in an office. You need to be out and about doing, fixing, creating, or making.

HIGH FLYER

You love a challenge, thrive under pressure, and have your sights set on achieving great things. The world is your oyster, but don't expect success to automatically lead to happiness. You should enjoy what you do, too.

ACADEMIC OR ACADEMICALLY to be focused on your studies

ADRENALINE-RUSH release of hormones that rushes blood around your body and makes you ready for action

APPROACHABLE someone who others can easily approach and talk to

CATALYST something or someone that causes a reaction or change

CLICHE action that is spoken about or seen so many times that it has become worn out and commonplace

CLIQUE small and exclusive group of friends that does not easily accept others into the group

CONFRONT OR CONFRONTATIONAL be ready to accuse, confront, or oppose something or someone. A confrontational person is someone who is quick to jump to their own or others defense or will attack something if they don't agree.

CONSCIENTIOUS take great pride in and care over your work

DYSLEXIC person who suffers from word blindness, and as a result has trouble reading. It is a disability and not something caused by low intelligence.

EXPECTATIONS things hoped for or expected. A parent's expectations are the hopes and dreams they have for their children or what they expect their children to achieve.

GRAVITATE be drawn to something or someone

HIERARCHICAL structure or system where power is at the top and descends downward

MANIPULATIVE be clever, skillful, or devious in getting others to do what you want them to do. To influence someone in an indirect or underhand way.

NICHE place or position that particularly suits someone

PAY DIVIDENDS gives you something extra

PRINCIPLED have high standards of personal conduct and morals

RETALIATION try to pay back some kind of wrong doing or injury

RIDICULE mocking behavior intended to embarrass and humiliate someone

SELF-ESTEEM respect for yourself. To have self-esteem is to think favorably about the person you are and to be happy with your achievements or the way you behave toward others.

SYMPATHETIC OR SYMPATHY show understanding toward one another

WHIMS fleeting and often fanciful thoughts

THE GET REAL ADVICE DIRECTORY

If you've got a problem and you'd like to talk to a trained professional or counselor, here are some useful numbers. Don't suffer in silence. These help lines are there to help you and you don't have to give your name.

HELP LINES

Al-Anon/Alateen 1-800-344-2666

Child Help USA 1-800-422-4453
Child abuse hotline for victims, offenders, and parents.

National AIDS Hotline 1-800-342-AIDS

National Center for missing and exploited children 1-800-843-5678

National Runaway Hotline 1-800-231-6946
Operates 24 hours. Provides information, referral, and transportation back home for runaways.

National Suicide Hotline 1-800-SUICIDE

Teen Hotline 1-877-786-7846
Emotional advice for young people.

Youth Crisis Hotline 1-800-448-4663

FURTHER READING

Ayer, Eleanor H. *Teen Smoking*. San Diego, Calif.: Lucent, 1998.

Goldentyer, Debra. *Child Abuse*. Chicago: Raintree, 1998.

Goldentyer, Debra. *Divorce*. Chicago: Raintree, 1998.

Peacock, Judith and Jackie Casey. *Depression*. Mankato, Minn.: Capstone, 2000.

Ruiz, Ruth Anne. *The Dangers of Binge Drinking*. New York: Rosen, 2000.